TRAILS
OF
TEXAS

TRAILS
OF
TEXAS

by William B. Ruggles

The Naylor Company
Book Publishers of the Southwest
San Antonio, Texas

To My Wife

DOROTHY SHERIDAN RUGGLES

Whose cooperation and incentive have made possible this
anthology of verse, the compilation is dedicated

On Our Wedding Anniversary

A year of yours, a year of mine are rounded out today —
We've stepped a little further on along the broad highway.
And if the step has slowed a bit, for that we do not pine,
So much we see who slowly tread a year of yours and mine.

A year of yours, a year of mine! And not without its tears,
But bright the sunlight gaily glints to color hopes and
    fears . . .
Tomorrow beckons down the road, through leaves the
    sunbeams shine
And gay we face the morrow of a year of yours and mine.

PREFACE

Looking back over eighty years of life, I can recall having written verse since my early boyhood. The Fredericksburg, Virginia *Star*, then edited by Connor Goolrick, a cousin of my father, printed two of my poems in 1901 when I was ten. In the next nine years, my contributions had voluminous publication in the Austin, Texas High School *Comet*, in *The Magazine* of The University of Texas, its literary monthly, and the student annual, *The Cactus*. At nineteen, I entered the newspaper business as sports editor and dramatic critic of the Houston *Post* and for the next fifty years, 1910-1960, served Texas journalism continuously with the *Post*, 1910-1916, the Houston *Chronicle* one month in 1916, The Galveston *News*, 1916-17, The Dallas *News*, 1919-1925 and again, 1926-1960. Since retirement that last year, I still as editor emeritus, contribute to The Dallas *News*. Actually I was in World War I service, 1917-19, World War II, 1942-46, which The *News* regards as on leave of absence. There have been two breaks in service with The *News*, six months in 1920 when I was executive secretary of the Dallas Automobile Club, and 1925-26 when for a year I was executive secretary of the Ex-Students Association of The University of Texas. As a consistent moonlighter, I was associated with the Texas Baseball League from 1920 to 1961 as its official statistician, 1921-25 as its secretary and for most of 1929 as its acting president.

Throughout this period, I maintained my interest in writing poetry and estimate that I have published over 3,000 verses. Most of this was written for various daily columns that I authored for the three newspapers for which I wrote sports, 1910-1925, later for columns used at different times and under various pseudonyms and aliases for the editorial page of The Dallas *News*, including a daily one, 1950-51, "Out of the News" as "The Newsman" and for which I wrote fully half of the verse and prose under nearly a score of different names, never my own. For two years, 1916-17, at the instance of the late John Avery Lomax, I wrote "Bill Ruggles' Colyum" for the *Alcalde*, the monthly magazine of the Texas Exes, wrote extensively for it, including unsigned poetry, in my year as secretary, and wrote its editorial page, 1926-41. During my World War I service, I was for a time the editorial writer for the Third Army's daily newspaper in Coblenz, *The Amaroc News* and also wrote a daily verse for it under the title "Studies in Nude Life," signed "W.B.R. 28th Infantry." Also during my year with the Ex-Student Association, 1925-26, the *Austin Statesman* syndicated in Texas a column of sports comment I wrote daily.

In 1936-37, Lynn Landrum, editorial editor of the *Evening Journal*, then the sister publication of The *Dallas Morning News*, enlisted me as one of several News-Journal staff writers of verse and a few outsiders, to contribute one poem each week to his page. For the Texas Centennial year, 1936, I conceived the idea which resulted in the series of historic poems which introduce this volume, using the overall title which is used for this anthology, *Trails of Texas*.

In selecting for this anthology, general interest, rather than the specific represented by sports writing, has been kept in mind.

William B. Ruggles
Dallas, Texas
May 1, 1971

CONTENTS

WAR

TRAILS OF TEXAS

I.

CONCEPCIÓN

Along Camino Real, the wild Apache strays . . .
Before the Mission's altar, the good Franciscan prays
For souls of foe and brother. So run the Mission's days.

Gone is Fra Santa Ana, the red man long since fled,
The men of Spain in armor are numbered with the
    dead . . .
Concepción, still brooding, survives in all their stead.

The human mind envisions the power it may attain . . .
Always it is forgetting life can but wax and wane —
Here in the quiet sunlight the works of God remain.

II.

SAN JOSÉ

Without, the wooded stretch of hinterland
Knew threat of danger from a savage race . . .
These Mission walls held out a pitying hand
And promised peace within their cloistered space.

Today the crowding city hems them in,
Yet for all that bustle, clamor never cease,
The graying Mission shuts without the din . . .
Within is quiet and an age-old peace.

III.

PIONEER

He could not breathe in a crowded place —
He wanted his air and his open space.
He watched while civilization neared
On the path through the wilderness Boone had cleared,
Saw highways hiding the Indian trails,
Heard engines pushing their way on rails.
The prairie called to the listening ear
And the restless foot of the Pioneer.

He whistled to his dog and called to his wife,
Loaded his rifle and sharpened his knife,
Tossed in a wagon a pan or two,
Texas bound — to a land plumb new.
They watched him go and shook each head . . .
"Shiftless fool! Better stay," they said.
Not a sign they saw that might denote
That a Nation rode in his coonskin coat.

IV.

COVERED WAGON

The dust cloud rose from the prairie,
Ever the four wheels turned,
The ruts new trails to the westward
Where the blazing sun rays burned . . .
Somewhere beyond the skyline
There would be rest and peace,
Home in a newer homeland,
And the wheels at last could cease.

Life is a covered wagon,
Endlessly pushing on,
Our hopes and our fears beside it,
Our dreams of a newer dawn . . .
Each of us pioneering
On and on to the West —
Somewhere beyond the skyline,
We shall come at last to our rest.

V.

MOTHER OF A RACE

Into the West strode the Pioneer, hardy and bold and strong,
And wherever he drove his wagon team, his woman went
    along;
Maybe she liked the place they left and feared for the dark
    before —
That worn-out farm that wouldn't produce, she'd have
    given it one chance more . . .
But he wanted to go, so go they did — the print of their
    trail is dim,
But a nation rose in the wake of their steps, because she
    went with him.

We honor the venturesome breed that won from the wilder-
    ness the West,
Who tilled their farms in the war-whoop's dread with a
    musket held at rest,
Who tracked the forests and blazed the trails that led to the
    Gulf and the sea,
And after they staked a new-found land had to fight to make
    it free . . .
But only a woman makes a home — their deeds would
    disappear,
Were it not for the woman who went along, the Wife of the
    Pioneer.

VI.

THE ALAMO
(March 6, 1836)

Before the Mexicans' advance, our people fled dismayed . . .
Our food was scant, our numbers few, ill-armed, and — yet —
    we stayed,
Our fortress but the crumbling walls where once the priests
    had prayed.

Our outposts could not hold in check six thousand of the
    foe . . .
They took the town . . . We held our fire, our powder
    running low . . .
Hemmed in two hundred Texans stood to hold the Alamo.

Then Travis called. We heard his voice above the cannon's
    din:
"Shall we give up a post," he asked, "our comrades died to
    win?
Shall we haul down a dauntless flag and let the Mexicans
    in?"

Behind us home and hope and love, fields where our chil-
    dren played —
Before us, rank on threatening rank, the heartless foe
    arrayed —
A thousand might have held our walls, but our two hundred
    stayed.

"No quarter!" signed their blood red flag. We heard their
    bugles call.
All day their grim battalions came — we beat them from the
    wall.
All day our stubborn rifles spoke — their bravest charged to
    fall.

All night our helpless wounded groaned. We saw the watch
    fire's glare.
We heard the sentinel's challenge round upon the midnight
    air . . .
For all we held the pack at bay, we knew the wolves were
    there.

One dawn their cannon breached the wall . . . the rifle's
    crack replied . . .
We saw Castrillon's columns form and waited, death be-
    side,
Loaded again our smoking guns and envied those who
    died . . .

*　*　*　*　*　*

Go — drive around the Plaza now — the walls still stand
    today —
On the old Chapel's hallowed ground the peaceful sunbeams
    play
Where theirs to choose was life or death. They chose —
    and there they stay.

VII.

GOLIAD

(March 27, 1836)

Drip — drip — drip from the pile of dead
Spreads the blood in the sod of Goliad.

Truce from battle, rest from fight —
Prisoners — true, but their hearts are light —
Hushed is the rifle, sheathed the sword
On the plighted faith of the Mexican's word.
On the huts where they lie shines a red moon down,
On captor and prisoner in Goliad town.
A banjo strums of a Georgia home —
Young feet shuffle on alien loam.
Ominous shadows streak the ground
In the long night march of the sentry round.
Never a shadow falls athwart
The hope that springs in the captive's heart.
Tomorrow — Georgia bound — they said,
Home from the huts of Goliad.

The red moon sank as the sun rose red,
Red as that day in Goliad.

Laugh and jest as the ranks are led,
Double file, from Goliad.
"See you in Georgia!" — spirits high —
How could they know that they marched to die?
Sombre death stalked all unseen
With the stern-faced men that they marched between.

10

Jest and laugh — for youth is gay —
The wounded hobbled along the way,
But what is a broken bone or two,
When you're going back to the home you knew?
"See you in Georgia! . . . Home next! . . . God!"
As the shattered breast smeared the bloody sod.
Shriek and scream where the jest had stirred
As the muskets crashed to the murderer's word.

Drip — drip — drip from the pile of dead
Spreads the stain of blood through Goliad.

Dust in the dust of Goliad
Lie the nameless ranks of the slaughtered dead.
Nor slab nor column stands to tell
The world they knew of the way they fell.
Their monument is a Nation's rise —
A single star in a Nation's skies.

Drip — drip — drip through the years will spread
The blood of the men of Goliad.

VIII.

THE WARD AND FANNIN DEAD
(March 27, 1836 — March 27, 1936)

Where Goliad had caught them to her breast
A hundred years ago, today they lie . . .
In pride eternal Texas guards their rest
Who showed so well they knew the way to die.

The path of glory they had followed through
Dead end at Goliad, they thought, it showed —
How wrong they were who, falling, never knew
They blazed a trail up which a Nation strode.

IX.

PLACID RIVER
(April 21, 1836)

Gently flows the placid river
Into San Jacinto Bay.
In the east the dawn is breaking
And the gray mists fade away . . .
Santa Anna! Santa Anna!
Know you not that it is day?

Look! The camp of Houston stirring
'Neath your batteries' gloomy frown —
There are but eight hundred rifles,
There were less in Bexar town,
When the Alamo blazed glory
Till sheer numbers bore it down.

Still the placid river's flowing
And the day is hastening on —
Beyond, high noon — siesta —
Do you hold your foes to scorn?
Santa Anna! Santa Anna!
Lo! Your golden chance is gone!

Where the placid stream glides gently
On its way into the bay,
Some will wake to bloody vengeance,
Some will never wake today,
As the might of Texas, risen,
Sweeps the tyrant host away!

X.

SAN JACINTO
(April 21, 1836)

Seven hundred Texans are marching down the river,
Scrambling through the brushwood and heading for the
    sea,
Before them is the ocean and behind them Santa Anna,
Houston at the head of them, a Nation to set free.

The ghosts that held the Alamo are marching in the
    ranks . . .
The blood that flowed at Goliad is seeping down the
    banks . . .
The stoutest heart may falter, the weakest urge to fly,
For behind them is the Butcher and a crimson in the sky.

Seven hundred Texans have halted where the Bayou,
Wedded to the river forms an angle at their back:
History starts to writing the name of San Jacinto
As seven hundred Texans get ready to attack.

And now the charge is sounding the Texans to the fray . . .
The bridge is down on Vince's path — they fight or die
    today —
They storm the works . . . They take the camp . . . They
    rout a frantic foe —
They have snatched a tooth for Goliad, an eye for Alamo.

Seven hundred Texans down a hundred years go march-
    ing —
A Nation grown behind them where its flag they first un-
    furled
Keeps in everlasting glory for that day at San Jacinto
The single star they blazoned to the gaze of all the world.

14

XI.

EWIN CAMERON

(Huehuetoco, Mexico, March 27, 1843)

They have halted Ewin Cameron by the hut's adobe
wall . . .
They have tied his arms behind him and they wait the
bugle call . . .
They have brought a priest to shrive him and a bandage for
his sight,
He'll march no more with men of Mier nor sleep in chains
tonight.

Then speaks up Ewin Cameron: "Your priest I do not
need —
I will answer to my Maker to His face for every deed . . .
And take away your bandage — I would look death in the
eye.
What Highland heart has faltered when the time has come
to die?"

Far away is Santa Anna, cringing in his butcher's den —
Fearless stands there Ewin Cameron, hero soul and man
of men . . .
Gallant Scot who died for Texas, still your valiant deeds
inspire —
Brave you faced those murderous muskets and yourself
gave word to fire.

XII.

HOOD'S BRIGADE
(1861-1865)

(Jefferson Davis to the Texas regiments of the
Army of Northern Virginia: "The men of other
states have their reputation to make, but the sons
of the Alamo have a reputation to maintain.")

Reared to the war-whoop,
    Rousing at night,
Bred to the rifle,
    Dauntless in fight,
Through four grim years of hell,
    Bold, unafraid,
Marches with Robert Lee
    John Hood's Brigade.

"Men of the South have
    Fame yet to gain,
Sons of the Alamo,
    Theirs to maintain!"
Richmond and Sharpsburg —
    How their foes fled,
Still they maintained it,
    Living and dead!

Never their glory dimmed!
    Still how it awes,
Furled though their dauntless flag,
    Ended their cause!
Still are their laurels green,
    Never to fade —
Third, Fourth, Fifth Texas —
    Hood's old Brigade!

XIII.

THE RANGER

Once along the border, like the drift of autumn leaves,
Thronged the Indians, desperadoes and the cattle-lifting
    thieves
Until there came swift-riding over the valley, hill and flat
The Law in dirk and derringer and tall — white — hat.

Rip Ford and old Buck Barry — there is glamor in the names
Of the men who made the Rangers, as the record still
    proclaims:
The lifter left the cattle and the outlaw hid his gat
When they thought about the rider in the tall — white —
    hat.

As tall as he his story from the borderland uncouth —
Some of it is legend but most of it is truth . . .
For fact stands out of hard fought fight, or years of stand-
    up strife —
The Ranger rode the border and the outlaw rode for life.

His is a tale unended. Still riding down the years
Come the hoofbeats of the Ranger and his stalwart form
    appears . . .
Though dark may be the danger, he has no care for that,
Riding on into the future in his tall —white — hat.

XIV.

LONGHORN

This is the song of the vanished cattle,
Gone from the range where they held their way,
Crowded out of the hurrying battle
By finer breeds of an easier day:
Monarchs they were when they roamed the ranges
Or plodded far on the Chisholm Trail . . .
On came Time, with his moods and changes —
The Longhorn breed — it had to fail.

What has become of the ghostly riders —
Chapped, sombreroed — the Longhorns knew?
Their place has gone to their day's outsiders,
They and the Longhorns both are through!
The King of the Plains — in a zoo you find him,
Bones of his brothers bleach in the sun —
His wide eyes stare at a past behind him
And the Longhorn's long, long day is done.

XV.

CATTLE

They saw the Old West ride away —
They watched the dawn of a newer day,
When the plains were fenced and the Red Man gone
And sombreroed cowboys riding on . . .
They stood — and there they stand and wait
For what may come with the call of fate.

So it has been since the world began,
For all the pride of the Adam man:
His works are gone and his very name
In the dust is buried whence it came,
While the dumb and driven beasts anon,
As they served the father, serve the son.

XVI.

ALIEN

Not less their loyalty is ours who still
Look back with tenderness on whence they came,
And keep alive in memory the past
In hearts, the hearth for an undying flame;
Who bring from Rhine and Danube and blue Rhone
The ancient customs of their fathers' loam,
Quaint costumes, quainter tales of gnome and elf,
Quaint dances from that other, distant home;
Who sing again the dream songs of their land
And pass its tongue from father on to son,
That older happiness may form a link with this
New happy freedom in a new land won.

XVII.

ETERNAL ARMISTICE

(For the Fallen Foe)
1918

They had no part where the wars were making,
Who ere the ink on the scrolls had dried
Marched in youth to the cannon's shaking,
Who faced the flame — and dared — and died.

There are no foes where the bugles' blowing
May not break on the dreamless sleep
Of those who lie 'neath the poppies growing
In the silent fields that the dead men keep.

There is no creed, no hate of races,
Beyond the spell of the common sod,
When they come home from the scattered places
To plead their cause at the throne of God.

XVIII.

THE DRAFT

(1917-1925)

They had known the feel of the shovel. They had swung
    with the ax and the pick,
They had held the plough in the furrow and dodged to the
    old mule's kick.
They had heeded the factory whistle. They had chauffered
    and clerked and mined,
Till they heard the call of the bugle and they left those
    lives behind.

Then in the vat they were melted and then they were poured
    in the mold,
While the furnaces roared about them in a world grown
    strange and old,
Where Thor in his fiery smithy, back to his trade again,
Hammered and shaped and fashioned and laughed as he
    made them — men.

And now they are back to the shovel, to the factory, ax and
    pick,
To the endless line of the furrow, the plow and the old
    mule's kick.
And those who were not broken, who came unscathed
    through the flame,
Know that the world about them will never be quite the
    same.

XIX.

REVIEW

Palacios, Texas, August 16, 1935
(For Maj. Gen. John A. Hulen)

The long lines stiffen to the shout
Of sharp command. In ranks they wheel . . .
"Pass in review!" — The squads move out . . .
Bright glint the slanting lines of steel.

Your eyes behold another day
And other youngsters marching in,
Who kept the faith their Texas way
And hold the ground they died to win.

"Eyes — right!" Still comes the olden thrill . . .
To "Front!" — so ends your last review . . .
Bright flames today the spirit still
Of those who marched and fought with you.

XX.

ARMISTICE

(1918-1938)

"There will be peace," they said, "when we have paid
The final price." They bravely flung aside
Their youth and dreams. "This is our gift — " they said,
"A warless world." . . . And in the flames they died.

"We will be gone," they said, "when dawn shall break
On carefree lands no burst of horror stuns —
At peace because we died." Their old graves shake
To the steady rumble of the front-bound guns.

XXI.

CENTENNIAL YEAR

(1936)

Laughs the stout Conquistador with blood upon his glove,
Shrills the scalp-locked Red Man with menace in his cry,
Chants the gray Franciscan of a message that is love —
All are ghosts together as the years go hurrying by.

Rides Almonte's Lancer — in his green and yellow gay,
Cocks an ear the Ranger for the sound of hostile fire,
The Pioneer comes planting and the Rebel has his day —
All the gallant shades of them to make the heart beat higher.

Spectral now the wigwams and the cabins on the plain . . .
A newer Texas rises by river, gulf and lake . . .
But from the past comes thronging to greet with us again
A hundred years of Texas that the ghosts all helped to make!

XXII.

ALAMO REPLICA

(Texas Centennial Exposition, Dallas, 1936)

Touch the doors and touch the wall,
Symbol of old stalwarts' fall.

Here is inspiration drawn
From Texas heroes, dead and gone.

A copy, yet upon its face,
The older Alamo we trace!

Those who died, but not in vain,
With us cannot live again.

In replica, their spirit still
Goes marching on and always will.

PINE WOODS CHURCH

No high cathedral heart have I
For chancel, nave and aisle,
For chanting choir and towering spire
Of consecrated pile.

For mine is but a simple faith
In ways my fathers trod
And humbly rise to friendly skies
The prayers I make to God.

XXIV.

FOR GOV. JOHN CONNALLY
(November 22, 1963)

Death rode beside you in our tragic hour,
    Death struck, drew back, withheld his fatal blow . . .
Your people thank His hand, whose wondrous power
    In gentleness and mercy willed it so!
Men rise and serve who know the Nation's need,
    Aware that they in serving so may fall;
The patriot, trusting not in words but deed,
    Dares danger, death itself, at country's call.

We mourn our leader, stricken at your side —
    Felled by a coward's bullet, he is gone . . .
God spared you and you live — we turn in pride
    To know that you will lead us bravely on!
For state, for country, there is work to do —
Texas and the future turn to you!

———

(Note: This poem was written at the request of the Texas Bank and
Trust Company of Dallas, as part of a presentation to him in the wake
of the Governor's wounding by the assassin of Pres. John F. Kennedy at
the time the latter was killed.)

MARCH 2

(March 2 is of course Texas Independence Day
and adopted as its own by The University of Texas
that makes it an occasion for students and alumni
to sit down and break bread together wherever in
the world two or more Exes or Alumni may happen
to meet. Original inspiration was March 2 in
Brisbane, Australia. It was rewritten for March
2, 1950, eight years after its 1943 start.)

A clatter of hoofs in the dark night sky, the saddles creak
    and strain,
And Texas calls, as the riders pass, the roll of her sons again:
Look left! Look right! Where the years have trod, the print
    of their trail is there!
Look right! Look left! They are marching on by the earth
    and the sea and the air —
The breed that battled the Mexican back, that tamed Co-
    manche pride,
That followed Lee and Beaumont Buck . . . Now in their
    sons they ride!
And Tunis hills have heard their call, Italy's known their
    tread,
As the sons of Texas faced the tasks that were faced by her
    mighty dead.

    Texas! Texas! There they go
    On the long brave road from the Alamo —
    Travis beside a Texas lad,
    Bowie with one in khaki clad,

> Another Houston, a new Lamar,
> The fighting sons of our own Lone Star!
> The world has warmed to your campfires' glow
> Texas, wherever your Texans go!

Voices rise from the long, long trail, the trail that has led
    so far . . .
Look left! Look right! Through the gathering years, you
    know where their pickets are!
San Jacinto's few look down and know that the breed is good
Where the men of New Guinea's glades looked back to cheer
    to the men of Hood . . .
By sniper's nest and pillbox threat, the newer breed went
    on
When the Jap gave back from the bayonet in the grip of a
    Texas son . . .
Far cry it was from the men in gray who charged on the
    Devil's Den,
But the breed dyed Anzio Beach in red with the blood of
    our fighting men.

> Texas! Texas! There they go,
> Your sons on a trail so well they know —
> Texas river and Texas plain
> And Texas farm in the ranks again:
> Texas blood and Texas brawn
> Carrying Texas on and on!
> Where by desert and forest lurk the foe,
> Texas! Texas! There they go!

Look left! Look right! As the years go on, our shadowy
    riders smile:
From Goliad to Faid Pass is many a hard-fought mile . . .
A Ranger laughs as he wipes a brow that is red from the
    bullet's crease
And waves to a Texas lad whose plane rode flaming down
    to peace . . .

Each gap was filled, as the gaps are filled, by men who stand
    to their guns
When Texas raises her battle cry and calls to her fighting
    sons . . .
And Texas mourns each falling file, but proudly lifts her
    head
To watch their comrades face the tasks that were faced by
    her mighty dead!

> Texas! Texas! There they go,
> Wherever needed to strike a blow!
> The Texas heart goes surging still
> Down flaming valley, up gun-rimmed hill!
> Whatever the odds, wherever the field,
> No task has daunted the men you've steeled
> (Not a man held back in the Alamo!) —
> Texas! Texas! There they go!

WAR

SOISSONS

(July, 1918)

(Moving northward from Paris towards Soissons
in July, 1918, men of the First Division, American
Regulars, saw true mistletoe growing against the
stocky trunks of the willows.)

The road was a trackless pathway, hid in the murky light —
The dawn was a sable daughter, born of the womb of night —
The wind of morn was a whisper down from the ashen sky
    But they saw on the trunks of the willows,
    The ghastly trunks of the willows,
"Mother of God!" said the Sergeant, "mistletoe — in July!"

There hung like jewel carving clusters of gray and green —
The dew on the pearl-drops glistened where the kiss of the
    dawn had been —
The thin stripped limbs of the willows swung in the dawn-
    wind's breath,
    Cold and chill in the morning —
    The footsteps marched to the morning —
"Mother of God!" said the Sergeant, "the gray is the hue
    of death!"

They saw it an eerie warning from the pagan mistletoe,
Nodding against the helmets of the men who marched
    below —
Man after man by the willows where the weird gray witch-
    balls swung
    With the wind of dawn in the clusters,
    Reading death in the clusters,
Death in the wheat fields lurking where the murk of the
    morning hung.

THE GUNS COME HOME

(When we of the 1st Division came home in 1919,
we left behind the 2nd Battalion of the 6th Field
Artillery, which had gone through the war from
1917 on. The unit was not relieved from the Army
of Occupation until April 22, 1921.)

Old Ehrenbreitstein's frowning shadows fade —
Slow dies the echo of the rushing Rhine —
The guns come home, the guns whose thunder played
The marching music for the Yankee line.

No more the caissons roll along the way
Where long battalions of the old First wound —
The silent muzzles can but dream today
How, foot by foot, the stubborn foe gave ground.

They speak no more in flame o'er Cheppy dell
Nor frown across the Soissons right of way
Nor bathe the steep slopes of Mont Sec in shell —
No Argonne drifts re-echo to their bay.

Cantigny to Sedan! They marked the trail,
A blood-bathed way across the death-strewn loam —
And now they wait to hear the friendly hail
That tells the path has led, at last, to home!

A.E.F.

(November 11, 1925)

It is far that we have wandered from the cobblestones and
     highways —
A thousand years to seaward are the crosses and the rain,
The battered streets and houses that were once our marching
     byways,
But when November swings around these live for us again.

We thought we had forgotten when "Retreat" the bugles
     sounded
And the caissons' farewell rumbled on the roads along the
     Rhine,
But the hail of unseen legions holds our heartbeats still
     impounded
As November brings the memory of the mates of yours
     and mine.

Where the tiny rain-washed crosses mark the places where
     they're sleeping
To hold our final outpost, November calls us yet . . .
Till we hear the Final Muster and the silent years come
     creeping,
The tie is there to hold us and we never shall forget.

DECORATION DAY, 1921

From Amarillo's wind-swept plain —
Beside Red River's flow,
They laid aside the tasks they knew
Who heard the call to go . . .
And now by Marne and Ourcq and Aisne,
Their endless post they keep
Where glory sheds her tears above
Adventure's final sleep.

The frowning height of Montfaucon
Is a headstone for the slain —
Lads sleep by Aisne who will not see
The Brazos rise again —
Perhaps upon some slumberer's sight
The Neches rice farms gleam —
Of yellow fields of Texas corn,
Perhaps today they dream.

God rest you, gallant gentlemen,
Who fared so far from home
To hold with dauntless Texas hearts
A strip of alien loam!
White fields of cotton blossoms still
Recall your lands of play —
God rest you well, our Texas lads,
Who gave your youth away.

A CHRISTMAS THOUGHT — 1921

Was it yesterday we heard it or a distant Christmas morning
When the green tips of the cedar boughs bent o'er a lad at
    play,
The tiny drumsticks beating on a toy drumhead at dawning
As the little toy battalions formed their ranks on Christmas
    Day?

> O! red the holly berries were
> Upon the youngster's sight —
> And Mary keep them red for him
> In Cheppy glen tonight!

All day the toy battalion marched — we heard the toy drum
    beating
Till the little hands grew weary and drooped the little head
And slumberland rose up at last to fondle him in greeting
And mother love tucked in the quilts around the little head.

> No mother hand may soothe his rest,
> The meed he won in fight,
> But Mary grant the snow lies warm
> In Cheppy glen tonight!

WILDING

(Anthony Wilding, the English and International
Tennis Star, was killed in the Dardanelles Cam-
paign, 1915.)

Only a name from the chosen dead
But straight to the world's sad heart it sped —
"Killed in action at duty's call —
The wonderful Wilding's dead" — that's all:
Scarcely a line of type to tell
How or where at the front he fell . . .
Only the fatal asterisk drawn
And a tear from the world for Wilding gone!

Gone? No never! For memory still
Recalls the game where he reigned at will —
Giant of body and great of soul,
Master of style — a royal whole . . .
Only the racquet's laid aside,
For only the shell of Wilding died —
The form we knew may be dead and gone
But heroic memory still lives on.

Lightly he leaped to his country's call,
Ready to live or ready to fall,
Just as old England's best have done,
Year after year, the sire and son,
Just as Picton and Wolfe and he
Who died that she still might rule the sea,
Just as her sons have always done,
Just as they will, till Kingdom come.

The weltering wave may form his grave,
"The watery wall" that he died to save,
But the world will forget the bursting shells
In a night attack on the Dardanelles —
The battle scene may fade for all,
But Wimbledon will his world recall
And his giant form with its swinging grace —
Goliath's body and David's face!

Wimbledon! There he reigned as king
Where the rhythmic stroke of his racquet's swing
Conquered the best at his chosen sport —
There Wilding, king, held his royal court . . .
French or Joffre themselves may fall
When death steps in with its tacit call,
But who would mourn for their spirits fled
As much as the world mourns Wilding, dead?

THE FIRST COMES HOME

First at the call of need to cross the foam,
Last to return of all, the FIRST comes home.
The FIRST! How proudly shines that honored name
In its place of right upon the scroll of fame!
First in the field and first to meet the foe,
First in the trenches, first to strike a blow
And first — the sad but proudest role of all —
To mark its chosen sons as heroes fall!
Their death their pride and ours, we greet today
The souls of Gresham, Enright and of Hay.
Adventurers three, your memory lingers best,
The slender Advance Guard on the pathway West!
The Hun who at Ansauville that sowing made
Has reaped the dragon's teeth — your debt is paid! . . .
First in all things but one, our trials are past —
The First Division greets its own at last!
Whose headlines flaunt their favorites' recall?
No state can claim us — we belong to all:
"Inch-deep-and-mile-wide" Powder River's pride
With Carolina's sons fought side by side;
And lads from Texas and the Kansas plain,
Shoulder to shoulder, marched with men of Maine —
In us the strain of all our land discern,
We went from all and now to all return!
We ask no tribute on this day of days.
Our efforts helped. Let others claim the praise.

For us enough our memories of our deeds —
Old days, old thrills that retrospect concedes;
Grim days of gas and shrapnel, march by night,
The barrage . . . the dawn . . . advance . . . the stand-up fight!
Old forms drift back through dreams of battle tide —
Brave men who lived and braver still who died!
Enough the enduring monument we have
Reared in the hearts of those who fought to save,
Enough for us the touch of native loam,
Enough that the first to go at last is — HOME!

The call goes out across the field — once more they come
   amain,
Where fullbacks smite a reeling line and tackles charge
   again . . .
Once more the interference forms to skirt yon husky end
Whose hurtling dive will give the best his strength can
   find to spend.

But schoolboy play! Yet these the ranks the country culled
   to find
So few years back the needed men to break the Kriemhilde
   line . . .
They little recked the bleachers' cheers, they did not ask
   for fame
Who found their best reward of all the glory of the game.

They found the paths through Argonne woods the Teuton
   blocked in vain —
They stormed the slopes of steep Mont Sec to drive him
   out again,
For just beyond the bullet hail that drenched the death-
   strewn way,
They saw the last white chalk mark loom, a touchdown on
   the play.

From grim Soissons to Montfaucon, past Cheppy's wooded
   aisles,
The Jerries, slowly beaten back by pressing Yankee files,
Could never know that those they faced across the fields
   of flame
Heard signals from a quarterback and — only played a game.

OLD ENGLAND SPEAKS

(At the 1924 Olympiad)

They start — they spring —
    They run — they leap:
I hear their cheers
    Who can only weep . . .
My runners lie
    By Ourcq and Aisne
Who will never start
    In a race again.

The oar-blade sweeps
    Through the silver blue —
The racquet swings
    As a drive comes through:
O crews and lads
    Of my land, white-bled —
From Mons to Marne
    Three million dead!

War calls the best
    And the best I sent,
The strong young grain
    To the ploughshare bent! . . .
They start — they spring —
    They run — they leap:
I hear their cheers
    Who can only weep.

1918 — CHRISTMAS — 1921

O little lights of Christmas-time that glow so red and bright
For those who will not come again shine out afar tonight
To where beneath their helmets sleep by brook and stream
    and run
The buddies that we left behind to hold the ground they
    won.

Along Cantigny's battered streets, astride the Soissons road,
The little crosses dot the path their weary footsteps strode;
Where Meuse and Moselle ripple on, they still keep watch
    and ward
The line they gave their lives to win their rusting rifles
    guard.

They loved the Yuletide customs once — the fireside's ruddy
    glow,
The holly green against the pane, the clustered mistletoe!
O little lights of Christmas-time, shine out across the foam
And give our buddies left behind another dream of home!

ON A COMRADE-IN-ARMS

(The citation on Georges Carpentier's award of
the médaille militaire reads: "Never returned with-
out having accomplished his mission." — James
Hopper.)

No more he heeds the brazen bugles' blowing,
No more he hears the rumble of the guns,
No more he sees the waving poppies growing
Where to the Meuse some hillside streamlet runs;
No more the handclasp as from friends he parted:
"Moonlight tonight! Beyond you is the Hun!"
The whirring motor of a mission started —
Not to return without that mission done.

That lies behind! Today amid strange faces,
He stands, defiant of the odds that loom —
Perhaps his thoughts go back to olden places
And he hears the bugles, calling through the gloom . . .
To silver notes again the air is trilling —
A task ahead and glory to be won —
Perhaps he hears again the mandate shrilling
Not to return without his mission done.

THE UNSEEN HOST
(May 30, 1926)

(Gresham, Enright and Hay, three enlisted men
of the 16th Infantry, First Division, were killed
in a German raid on the trenches at Ansauville,
the first casualties of the A.E.F. in 1917.)

From Ansauville, from Cheppy —
The echoes come again
Where once were raised the crosses
To mark the hallowed slain;
And once again — aye, once again —
The bugles sound to tell
How stubbornly the Yankee line
Avenged the brave who fell.

The chapel bells of Toul ring clear
Where once their muffled sound
Whispered of terror, stark by might,
The threat from Hun-held ground;
Scant earshot from the silvery peal
Beneath their helmets rest
The three who formed the slender point
For those who marched on West.

From Dun-sur-Meuse — from Belleau Wood —
Today is the message sped
To Argonne drifts that shelter now
The stacked arms of the dead;
No frowning cannon thunder now
Where still they hold the loam
They, living, won, but softly call
The bugle notes of home.

They may not know a world at peace —
So high a price they paid!
They may not see the mates they knew
Today on dress parade;
But when the bugles sound once more
Where the skies of home are fair,
Their shining souls are marching, too —
The Unseen Host is there!

THE CALL

(Dedicated to the First Division's initial Memorial
Reunion in Washington, D.C., October 3-5, 1922.)

They will not hear the bugles softly blowing,
They will not see the companies marching in —
The silent sentinel line that guards, unknowing,
The hallowed ground they gave their lives to win.

They will not see the old, familiar faces,
Renew the friendships formed in stirring days,
Who hold afar the tiny scattered places,
The final outguard of our battle days.

But when old memories crowd for us, still living,
They live again who fell along the line,
Cantigny to Sedan, their young lives giving
To push the Flag in earshot of the Rhine.

They are not dead . . . Their shining souls come winging
To answer Reveille with us again —
They are not dead . . . With memory living, bringing
The knowledge that they did not die in vain!

THE ADVENTURER

(This was written on learning for the first time in
1921 that an A.E.F. friend, Almeron W. Shanklin,
had been killed at Cunel in 1918, awarded a post-
humous D.S.C.)

Adventure called him from the beaten ways,
Fate to the plodding paths his footsteps tied,
And who could know he dreamed through placid days
He couched a lance by great Du Guesclin's side,
At Roncesvalles heard Roland's trumpet warn
And dared with Drake the peril of the Horn?

And then The Call! Four million of his kind
Drawn from their humdrum tasks afar from strife!
For him — romance! To petty hardships blind,
The bugle brought his crowding dreams to life —
Crecy and Poitiers! King Charles at Rheims!
Thor's hammer thundered in the Soixante Quinze!

They cursed the rain and mud. Clear-eyed, he saw
Beneath the Poilu's filth the heart below,
The faith that made "They shall not pass!" the law
That barred the pathway to the swarming foe,
Each farm the soul of France, and, unafraid,
Another Jeanne in every peasant maid!

July — Cunel — not all the crimson stain,
The widening splotch of red, the carmine streams,
The poppies lent amid the golden grain —
And so his soul went out in search of dreams.

*   *   *

Great heart! Naught now your gypsy soul may bar!
Tonight you strike the trail for what far star?

FAREWELL

(First World War victim from the field of International sport was Jean Bouin, French long distance runner who had established a world's hour record at Stockholm. An artilleryman, he was killed by a German shell September 29, 1914.)

Vale, Jean Bouin, no more on the cinder path
The world will behold the fast flash of your speed;
You who for France won the laurels of victory,
For France gave your life in her moment of need!
Vale, Jean Bouin, up the race course of heaven
Behind winged feet the long meters have spun . . .
Greater than triumphs at Paris or Stockholm
Is the chaplet of glory Jean Bouin has won!

LUCK

(Number 258 was the first drawn in the first U.S.A.
draft, 1917.)

"It's just my luck!" and he growled and frowned —
"I'm never around when a prize is won!
Two-Fifty-Eight is my number, and
Two-Fifty-Eight is Number One!"

"And I guess I'm lucky!" another laughed —
Youth through his laughter gold threads spun —
"Two-Fifty-Eight is my number, and
Two-Fifty-Eight is Number One!"

ACROSS THE TOP

The whispered word shall call them on
To the charge that death may stop—
In the cold, gray, sullen break of dawn,
They wait to cross the top.

Who knows what unseen dangers lie
Upon that strip of hell,
What comrades shall but charge and die,
What few will live to tell?

The deadly rush of pouring flame,
The pall of poisoned air,
The brave man's fear of craven shame—
All these are theirs to dare.

Death swings his waiting sickle bare
To reap his ripened crop,
But duty lies before them there
And they go across the top.

* * *

Crouched in the sheltered trench of fate,
Safe from the huge shells' drop
In youth's gray dawn of hope we wait
To cross the unseen top;

Nor know what terrors lie and loss
Where rolls the battle's strife
Nor who shall fall who charge across
The No-Man's Land of life.

But knowing deeds are ours to do,
The task we may not stop,
That glory waits the living few,
We go across the top.

FOR THOSE WHO PLAY

I do not hold that there is loss in play
And wasted time for life's pursuit of fame,
For I remember lads who went away
And cherished best the memory of a game.

Then when the gridirons back at home were bare,
Nor sun-baked diamonds stretched for them by day,
When frenzied stands could neither know nor care,
How well another game they learned to play!

JOHN POE — SOMEWHERE IN FRANCE

John Poe, you have left us, passed over at last,
Gone with the glamor that circled your name . . .
Heroic in retrospect, so you have passed —
Lovable vagabond, gone as you came . . .
Somehow we know that you laughed as you fell!
Cold you are lying there, somewhere in France —
Godspeed you, John Poe, for above you may tell
That still there are left to us days of romance.

Princeton remembers John Poe of old years —
Green were the laurels you won for her then,
Star of a game that in memory rears,
Monuments gray with the passing of men . . .
Vagabondia knew you, wherever a cause
Calls for a heart and a spirit of flame;
When the wanderlust gripped what were countries or laws
To a boy in whose soul still lurked joy in the game?

We had fancied them dead, those old chivalric days,
But the cold printed page has recalled them to view:
The helm of Navarre was but seen through a haze, —
Faint the Ironsides' cheer that old history knew —
Distant the age when the Cross charged the foe —
From a day that is gone gleams Du Guesclin's bright lance —
Somewhere in France you are lying, John Poe!
Thank God you brought back to us days of romance.

SPIRIT OF LIBERTY

"From Fontenoy — from Landen — the message
    runs again
Once more the fields of Flanders are strewn with
    Irish slain,
And once again, oh! once again, the heralds thrill
    to tell
How gloriously an Irish charge avenged the brave
    who fell."

                   — Alfred Gwynn

"What form shall freedom wear?" I heard. And as the
    message sped
Back through five centuries of space my hastening fancies
    fled
And proudly through the years I saw an Irish lad march by
Who wore the shamrock sprig and sang upon his way to die.

Cremona — Lille — Dunkirk and Ghent — who may their
    fame destroy
Who died with Sarsfield at Aughrim, with Clare at Fontenoy?
Beneath the blue and buff of Bourke there beat the Irish
    heart —
For faith, for freedom and for God, they played an Irish
    part.

For God! For Faith! For Freedom! What call would not
    they heed
If Right by numbers stood assailed or Liberty in need?
What if now England sounds the call? No Irish foot is late
While blazes still in Kerry — Clare — the soul of '98.

"The dust of some is Irish earth, among their own they
    rest" —
But, oh! how many, many more, the glorious and the best,
On foreign soil for freedom died and gave their souls to God
Far from the green of Irish earth, the shamrock and The Sod.

Shall Liberty the trappings wear of Amazons of old,
The trailing gowns of womanhood and locks of burnished
    gold?
For me the form of freedom seems a Paddy marching by
Who wears a shamrock sprig and sings upon his way to die.

THE SACRIFICE

Behind they leave their racquets
Behind, the bat and mask,
To learn another pastime,
To take another task;
They leave the rippling river,
Where Charles and Hudson flow,
When war its call is sounding,
The college games must go.

Oh, some will never hear again
The cheers from stands float free—
The roar of adulation
That greeted victory;
To greater fields they're marching
To play a greater game,
Where lives may pay for triumph,
Where death is meed of fame.

They dare, their lives who offer
When the flush of strength is by,
But what matters, old and broken,
The way we come to die?
Ah, theirs the greater courage,
The sacrifice in truth,
Who, marching put behind them
The playday of their youth!

TO EDWARD GRANT

(When a tablet to him was unveiled at the Polo
Grounds, Decoration Day, 1921. A captain in 77th
Division, A.E.F., Grant was the only major leaguer
killed in action in World War I.)

Behind us lie the years of world war battle . . .
We know no more the urge that drove us then,
But rises where the Unseen Host comes marching
An echo from the vale of silent men.

"We kept the faith!" no hint of grim reproaching,
Only upon the tranquil night air's breath
Rustles the echo of that last reminder,
Their challenge through the years: "We kept the faith!"

And still they keep it, as they lie there sleeping
By battered hamlet, road and ruined farm —
Here is the peace that passes understanding —
They kept the faith and could not come to harm!

THE SPORTING LEGION

"Fall in!" Whenever sounds the call —
The bugle's Reveille —
They leave the bat, the mask, the ball,
The tennis court, the tee . . .
The golfer drops his sticks at will,
The swimmer leaves his tanks,
While one and all march out to fill
The Sporting Legion's ranks.

Ask England how her sportsmen died,
And ask of France the same —
Their gentlemen were the first to ride
To war as to a game . . .
What mattered hopes and doubts and fears
With glory to be won?
From Mons to Marne, the world still hears
The Briton's "Carry on!"

"Fall in!" No patchwork squads shall stand
To tell a nation's shame . . .
Ah, no! To the sergeant's gruff command
Rings clear each answering name.
For lads once first the tape to break
Are drilling now with guns
Recruiters are quite glad to take
The Sporting Legion's sons.

1917

(This tribute to our men readying for action was
written for the sports page column of the Galveston
News in May, 1917, and was used on The Univer-
sity of Texas Commencement Program, June, 1917.)

No more from the quarter the signals are shrilling . . .
The players are gone and the gridiron is cleared . . .
No more to the struggle the bleachers are thrilling,
Never again will they cheer or be cheered . . .
Where the hoary gray walls of the college are aging,
Youths, free of care, they'll come never again —
In the crucible tried, where the battles are raging,
Those who return will come back to them — men.

Lightly they go with no thought for the morrow,
With a smile on their lips they are drilling today,
Lightly they go, but behind them is sorrow
For those left behind while they're marching away —
Behind for the harder task, watching and waiting,
With a prayer for the lad far away o'er the foam . . .
Lightly they go — there is no hesitating —
God guide them and guard them and bring them safe home.

MORT POUR LA FRANCE

(On the military cemetery at Ourches (Meuse),
France, written there in March, 1918.)

The red gods roared the challenge and they heard the
    bugles calling —
That mad Reveille their summons, aye, from half a world
    away —
Men were dying in the trenches, in the bloody shambles
    falling —
France had need of them — they knew it — was it time to
    watch and pray?
With the Hun unchecked in Flanders, should they wait to
    ask the way?

So they came without a question, for they heard a nation
    call them —
They had but their lives to offer and they gave these —
    to the flame,
To the gas, the wire, the shrapnel — ah, what horrors did
    befall them
Ere their souls, released, went winging to the haven whence
    they came!
Here the mortal part reposes until Michael comes to claim.

Softly fall the tears of heaven here upon them as they
    slumber
While the placid Meuse beside them croons its song of old
    romance,
Here they sleep till Judgment wakes them, through the
    years no man may number
They who braved the Great Adventure, they who took the
    Wondrous Chance,
They who heard the red gods calling and who gave their
    lives — for France!

(Note: All of those in the little cemetery on a small hill rising from the
banks of the Meuse were war dead. This verse was used to head an article
on the cemetery in the *Alcalde*. It was reprinted later in my column in
the *News*. Most of the dead in the cemetery had served in the Foreign
Legion or with the French Senegalese troops.)

PARIS
(Spring, 1919)

There are ugly things in Paris they see whose souls are blind,
Who never lift the curtain to seek the things behind —
The little glints of laughter, the thrills of fluted song,
Life's sunny little bypaths one may not travel long.

There are ugly things in Paris, they say who seem to seek —
Who look, unasked for find them, unbidden hear them speak;
Aye, ugly things in Paris, a city's painted lies,
Red revelry through flaming night, dawn in a harlot's eyes.

How should they see the sunlight whose very souls are
    blind —
Gay little shops and houses, gay little streets that wind,
The tiny bits of laughter, the thrills of fluted song
Life's sunny, happy bypaths one may not travel long?

Gold sunlight on the boulevards, a shop-girl's cheery smile,
A flower-maid selling posies — ah, many things worth-
    while! —
A crippled poilu passing, no sorrow in his face,
The merriest of children in parks of sunny space!

Old women at the market and gay throngs in the square —
Who thinks aught ill of Paris when Spring is in the air?
Old, courtly white-haired gentlemen who pause to bow to
      me —
Oh, wondrous things in Paris for those with eyes to see!

The little things of laughter, the thrills of fluted song,
Life's sunny little bypaths one may not travel long —
Oh, wondrous things in Paris for those who are not blind!
I saw them all in Margot's eyes the night the peace was
      signed.

A CANADIAN EXPEDITIONARY FORCE LEAVES FOR THE FRONT

"But the drum
Echoed 'Come! —
Death shall the braver harvest!' said the
sullen-sounding drum."

— Bret Harte "The Reveille."

Cheering thousands thrill the parting as the engine's sullen
breath
Gathers speed to bear them onward to the greedy maw of
death:
"For God — for King — for Country!" rolls the summons
of the drum
And the great Dominion answers to the Empire's call of
"Come!"

From the wheat fields of Alberta, from the great plains
sweeping free
From where Peace and Athabasca roar their passage to the
sea,
They have come to heed the calling, they have laid aside
the plough,
"We will answer England's summons," says the great
Dominion, "NOW!"

"Aye, we know the cost of harvest. We have harvested
before —
Ten survive for every hundred in the fallow field of war;
There is yet young grain left standing for the waving fields
we spent,
Though the sickle's swing played havoc with the ripened
crop we sent!"

"Our brothers went before us for the old Dominion's pride
And the ghosts of worn battalions tell the Empire how they
    died:
What is death beyond the moment of the shrapnel's shrieking
    roar?
Should we fear to go a-marching where so many marched
    before?"

"Shall we fear to join our brothers in Valhalla of the dead?
Shall we fear to follow after where their hero souls are sped?
By the graves of those departed, by their hearts that knew
    no fear,
When the Empire calls the muster, the Dominion answers
    'Here!' "

THE DOUGHBOY SPEAKS

"Give us one payday in Paris!"
Was our cry as we sailed from our shore,
"All the meed that we ask for our gay little task —
After that we will settle the score . . .
Then the piper we'll pay for his piping,
Clean up on the bills we have run!"
Now it's over, we're here. Those who're left lift a cheer
For the dance that we had with the Hun!
                    Now 'tis done —
He remembers the same, does the Hun!

The payday we longed for in Paris,
For a long time we had to forget
Along with the smiles and the feminine wiles
That adorn the Parisian coquette;
For a drill sergeant did all our piping
And it seemed he would never be done,
While for strathspey and prance, our only new dance
Was the one that we taught to the Hun
                    With our gun —
Oh, he danced to our pipes, did the Hun!

What a life! But who asked for a better?
There were thrills in the roll of the drum.
It was "Vive la vie!" when we came o'er the sea —
We were ready to help make things hum;
We asked but to get into action —
The quicker the better 'twas done —
There were scores we might pay and might God speed the
    day
When we stepped off our dance with the Hun!
                  Oh, the sun
Rose soon on our clash with the Hun!

And when "Taps" was the march for the number,
Grim tune, we'll concede, for the dance,
When a Bertha-made shell blew our fragments to hell
And they buried us — somewhere in France,
Light we strolled up to Peter, the keyman,
To tell him just how it was done,
That we died as we should and we counted it good
That we first had our dance with the Hun!
                    Even one —
Just one memorable fling with the Hun!

ON THE GREAT ADVENTURE

Whoso asked for glory, here upon the great adventure?
Whoso sought for fortune and whoso fared for fame?
With our feet upon the threshold of the drama spread
    before us,
Could we ask for greater triumph than the spirit of the
    game?

There were those that chose to linger (every other war
    has known them —
There will always be their brothers when the wars to come
    are through!) . . .
If they prospered in the turmoil, we can find no heart to envy
For they knew no winds that wander and their honey
    turned to rue.

They might walk their sheltered pathways, but we know
    it was not LIVING —
Ours alone that joy who knew it, tasting death from day
    to day . . .
Never theirs to know the friendship that survived the
    shrieking shrapnel
Nor the faces of our comrades as they fared into the fray.

Aye, for us the days sped onward. Death might meet us on
    the morrow,
As the lads at Ypres met it, singing grimly as it came . . .
They who stayed could have their hearthstones! Here was
    youth and life adventure!
Though hereafter comes disaster, we have lived and played
    the game!

LINES TO A RED CROSS GIRL

We were starving — second looeys do not draw a gob of pay
And are broke, like other mortals, as the long month wears
    away —
We were starving, really hungry, tottering on our looey legs
When you galloped to the rescue with your waffles served
    with eggs!

Waffles! In our dreams we'd seen them as one watches on
    the stage
Quaint creations represented, from some neolithic age —
Waffles! Brown ones, drowned in butter, smeared with
    syrup from the kegs!
And you served them, garnished nicely, with fried bacon
    and fried eggs!

Ah, aroma from Parnassus! Who would envy Jove his cup
Or imbibe ambrosial nectar on which gods Olympic sup,
While your waffle iron's waiting as you stir the batter by
And one's nostrils drink the perfume of a good old waffle
    fry?

Listen to us, Red Cross lady, while we pop the query old —
Would you like to have a hubby, one to cherish and to hold,
To come home stewed of evenings and to love you ever so?
Bring along your waffle iron — you can fill our bungalow!

———————

(Note: The waffles were real, served by a Red Cross friend in Coblens.)

IN APOLOGY

(Dear W.B.R.: I've read your lines on the Red
Cross, YMCA, KC, etc. Haven't you forgotten
there's a Salvation Army? — M.H.S. Doughboy.)

Faith, and we plead "Not guilty!" friend,
For if we failed to dash a rhyme
Ere this to grace that she might lend,
'Twas but to wait a better time . . .
Forget her? Not while doughnuts coast
Along our alimentary pass —
In their quaint incense, her we toast,
The OD clad Salvation lass!

Time was — ere we knew war and care —
We heard the old street-corner song,
Thin, quavering voices in the air —
We paused to smile, nor lingered long —
A jest, the echoing tambourine,
The clatter as the pennies came,
The rough crowd, gathered to the scene:
Now memory brings the blush of shame.

SHE never asked for song or praise —
SHE never paused to preach or rant —
For HER the same, black nights — red days —
SHE went ahead and, minus cant,

SHE took her hardships with the rest —
SHE ministered the way she knew:
And so her memory lingers best . . .
Dear maid, no one's forgotten YOU!

L'Envoi

Dear maid in OD, here's a line
From one unworthy to trespass —
Quaint charm and courage, faith divine,
Were one in you, Salvation Lass!

CAFÉ DE LA PAIX

From the Follies up to Maxim's and the Café de Paris,
There are Mademoiselles a-dancing though they hardly
    think of me,
But the lights are burning brightly and the boulevards they
    say
"Come you back, you Yankee soldier, to the Café de la Paix!"
To the Café de la Paix off the Avenue . . . and say!
If I ever quit the Army, I am going there to stay!
Oh, the Café de la Paix where the girls from Montmartre
    play —
It's never very lonely 'round the Café de la Paix.

She was neat and trim and dashing. She had curve and verve
    and style.
She could set you nearly crazy when she flashed her wicked
    smile.
She was walking with a Frenchy when I lamped her on a
    stroll,
But she ditched that helpless Poilu when I let her see my
    roll —
It was long back months of pay and I watched it melt
    away —
I spent it all in Paris but I don't regret the day
At the Café de la Paix . . .

I am sick of dodging M.P.s for these stolid fat frauleins
And the blasted wine and Moselle are the very worst of
    wines;
And I walk with Gretchen, Lena, but my heart is far away
(And they are not wearing stockings on the Boulevards, they
    say!)

Where you never see a Frau with a figure like a cow
But a girl just made for hugging and — believe me! — she
     knows how —
At the Café de la Paix.

Only ship me out of Prussia and I'll find my port of call
Where the old fizz stuff is bubbling and no one minds at all;
For the Boulevards are calling and the night lights burning
     free
And the old gang's at the Follies and it's there that I
     would be
At the Café de la Paix! Send me there without delay
Where the vermouth costs like sixty and you squander all
     your pay!
Oh, the Café de la Paix, where the girls from Montmartre
     play —
Oh, I hope up there in Heaven, there's a Café de la Paix!

———

(Note: The air of course is Mr. Kipling's "Mandalay." This verse was also
printed, postwar, in The University of Texas Ex-student magazine, the
Alcalde.)

IN MEMORY

"The years go fast in Oxford,
The golden years, and gay."
— Winifred M. Letts

The years go fast in Oxford,
The golden years, and gay
Perhaps as lovely now as once
Before they went away,
The careless lads who laid aside
For war their careless play.

The years go fast in Oxford . . .
It may be they forget
The carefree laughing voices.
Do they remember yet
The lads who doffed the cap and gown
And went — without regret?

The golden years of Oxford
Are fleeting still today
And still the hoary colleges
Look down on lads at play . . .
I love to think they best recall
The youth who went away.

REMEMBRANCE

Fraulein, your dancing eyes are bright —
Your smile is wondrous wine —
Your tresses stream in golden light —
You whisper you are mine:
All mine, you breathe — the stolen walk,
The kiss beneath the moon,
But I — I cannot soon forget!
Can you forget so soon?

Fraulein, twin azure pools your eyes,
But God! In them I see
Gray ground in Seichprey stretch where lies
A friend in agony —
The bloody trail through Argonne wood
No autumn leaves made red —
The crosses stark against the sky
Where lie the nameless dead!

Fraulein, your voice is fluted song
But through its thrill I hear
An echo rise from Louvain's wrong,
A maiden's scream of fear —
A widowed mother's anguished wail
Her starving child beside —
And groans that death was kind to still
Of gallant men who died!

All mine! — Your snow-white bosom's swell,
Your heart's hot throb divine,
The lure of you, your wondrous spell —
You whisper — all are mine!
But gray ghosts rise that will not rest
From far-flung trench and dune,
And I, Fraulein, cannot forget!
Can you forget so soon?